ADOPTION

EDUCATION

FOR EVERYONE

**For Adoptive Parents, Extended Family, Teachers,
Social Workers and More**

Brooke Fremouw

TABLE OF CONTENT

FOREWORD

It was nearly two decades ago when I realized that my family would not be growing in number through the traditional means of bearing children. My husband and I were married for years and ready to begin having children, only to learn that biological children would be difficult and expensive should we venture down that road. Through a series of ups and downs and a lot of struggle of "my will" vs "the Lord's will", our hearts were eventually opened up to the idea that our family would grow through adoption. Grief and pain that resulted from infertility had transformed into excitement for a new path that we had known little about.

What started out as an openness for younger children to come into our family, eventually turned into a desire for adopting children of all ages. Our vision of a life raising 4 children somehow turned into the reality of raising 11 children that we would call "ours" and an orphan care project (also serving impoverished children) in Ethiopia called Mission 10:10 (check us out at Mission1010.org), where many kids would lovingly call me "Mom".

Like my husband Jason and I, everyone that opens their hearts and homes to adoption starts on the journey for different personal reasons. Personal thoughts vary about the call to adopt and what the role of the adoptive parents 'is in answering that calling. Some adoptive parents jump in with little understanding of the Biblical truths around adoption. Other parents are drug across the start line by an eager spouse, not fully sure that the calling of their partner is truly a calling for themselves or their family. Infertility can become a catalyst for alternative ways for couples to raise a family. A lot of complexities can exist for couples that feel "forced" into adoption, rather than having the option of their "preferred idea" of growing a biological family of their own. There are also people in life that have not found their lifetime partner for marriage, but don't want to go through life without the blessing of raising a family of their own. Others may even be thrown into adoption through kinship placement (a family member in need of an adoptive home) or through being introduced to a child in need that simply melted a prospective parent's heart. Same sex couples choose adoption due to an inability to conceive between themselves. Foster care is another way that families can grow and transition into adoptive homes. No matter how adoption becomes the center of parenthood, there are fundamental understandings for both the adoptive parents and the people loving, supporting, or interacting with the adoptive family. As outsiders, we don't have to agree on the reasons that a person chooses adoption. Yet I do think we can all agree that whatever child is brought under the headship of an adoptive parent, that child is worth the time it takes to grow to understand them and best meet their needs as both a society and people interacting with the new family unit.

When my husband and I made the decision to adopt, we thought we knew what we were signing up for. Not unlike getting married, in which we had also thought we knew what would lie ahead in the months and years to come, adoption parenting is nothing like it is imagined to be. This is also true for ALL parenting, not just foster or adoptive parenting. One day, adults are responsible for themselves and the next day, they have a child that has to be the center of priorities in order for the child to develop properly. And though all parenting presents challenges and surprises, I can guarantee that the level to which the challenges exist in an adoptive family are exponentially higher and harder.

My husband and I were really fortunate that after our home study and licensing were complete, our family grew pretty quickly. Our first three children were all placed with us as infants and only 18 months apart. After we had several little munchkins running around, we then took in our first tween. The roller coaster ride of bringing in a tween was a lot. Despite how hard and painful it was for us parents, we knew more children were still in need of a home and we felt called to say yes to many more "older" children before receiving our last infant. All eleven of our children are not biologically ours, but very much ours all the same. We have kids from Ethiopia, kids from our home state in the US... we have fost-to-adopt children, birth mom placed children, a range of ethnicities, diversity in abilities and need levels, and an age range that spans 18 years between our oldest and youngest child. At the time of publication, we also have 7 incredible grandchildren despite our young age and the fact we are still parenting our own kids. Adoption has been a huge blessing in our home and hearts and if we could go back and choose to grow our family differently, we would not. Adoption was and will forever be the most painful and difficult thing we will endure on earth, and yet I would not choose to change it today even if I could. I am a better version of myself, I am more trusting and dependent on our Lord, and I am so full in my heart despite the many tears and fears that I continue to have to lay down. Adoption has been a huge gift and blessing to me.

This book was born out of necessity. As a Certified Trauma Support Specialist, I work with adoptive families from all over the country and some from across the oceans. I have countless experience with adoptive parents and adoptive children, both my own and those of others. The pains an adopted child feels and the source of those pains changes over the course of their childhood. The subtle and often well-intended ways in which a child receives messages from the world around him/her will impact the ways in which the child interprets their life and how much pain they unnecessarily have to muddle through. From our first outings when we received our children all those years ago, we quickly realized that the majority of society is unaware of the unique needs that adoptive families and adoptive children have. Many unknowing onlookers in the first year alone inflicted confusion, pain, and fear in our hearts and the hearts of our children. Our children still, nearly two decades later, are treated differently and see themselves differently than others because of their adoption stories and the ways in which society speaks to those differences. Let me share some things we have been told over the years that have a negative impact on our family and our journey:

"What is wrong with a mother that they would give their baby away?"

"Are you their real mom?"

"What a lucky kid to have a mom like you."

"Are these your son's real siblings?"

"Where is the child's birth mom?"

"Wow. That is so amazing. I could never do that. You guys are incredible."

Words aren't the only ways adoptive families hear messages of difference. Nearly all adoptive parents that have "survived the teen years" with their budding young adults will report that they feel misunderstood by their support systems, surrounded by people but alone, withdrawn from "normal" life with teens, and afraid for both what is and what lies ahead. Often it isn't just the words of the people around them that create these extreme feelings of isolation and judgement. Most times, the actions of others sends a clear message that the higher needs of many adopted children are too much for others to handle. Adopted parents feel guilty for the secondary trauma put onto extended family by the actions of the adoptee within the family and the difficulty it causes. Adoptive parents get "the look" when their children are so volatile and others feel that the disciplines are wrong or that the child was a "mistake to bring in".

The strangers at the stores, the teachers at school and church, the social workers on case plans, often even people on the therapeutic teams and the best intended friends and family members simply aren't familiar with the intricacies of adoption. The intentions behind the above statements tend to be good in nearly 100% of the instances in which they are said. Yet the outcome of speaking to adoptive families without specific adoption education is that inadvertently, a script is written in the hearts of both the parents and the children.

Adopted children have unique stories, unique perspectives and often come with neurodiverse bodies. Adoptive parents also have unique needs and perspectives on both family and life. I am a believer that when we "know better, we do better". This book is an attempt to help our well-meaning society and those interacting within the adoptive community to show up in ways that help adopted children feel supported, accepted, and cared for. The messages in this book can help the family and friends surrounding the adoptive parents to feel less alone in their differences and more accepted. This book is built from my life experience as an adoptive mom, orphan advocate, and Certified Trauma Support Specialist working with hundreds of families. It is meant to be given to teachers, family members, specialists, social workers, and even other adoptive families as they engage within "our world" as adoptive families. Adoption is difficult from the day we say "yes" until the day we leave this earth. It requires work to be approved, work to move a child into our family, work to create stability within the family, and work to help launch a child into adulthood. Having a compassionate team, society, friend and family system makes what is already difficult, a bit easier. If making the life of a hurting child and a knit-together family better requires only minor adjustments in speech and action, isn't that something we could all consider doing?

I hope you feel confident sharing this book with everyone in your circle in order that the adopted children in your life are loved in ways that help them reach their highest potentials. Several concepts may be repeated in basic mention from section to section, in order that the reader which chooses to only read the parts they feel most pertain to them, will not miss out on the ideas necessary for understanding. If you are reading cover to cover, which is definitely recommended, please be patient in the repetition. For more information on trauma informed care and the services rendered by Journey University for Adoptive Families and myself, Brooke Fremouw, please find me at TheTraumaMama.com, on Facebook @BrookeHosman-Fremouw or on Youtube at https://youtube.com/@all4Africa

CHAPTER 1

NOT BROKEN, AND DON'T NEED FIXED

I was so blessed that in the beginning of my story as an adoptive mother, I was able to receive three babies within 18 months of the time we took in our first little boy. I say that knowing that those babies coming into our home were the desire of my heart and NOT the desire of any of my babies ' hearts. And yet, years of infertility had me ready to change diapers and do late night feedings with a grateful heart. If infertility was not such a big part of my story, I am not sure what my gratitude would have looked like as these treasures were added to our home. Because I thought adoption was such a tremendous gift, I didn't understand why other couples would keep having biological baby after biological baby when they knew

1. How many kids were out there in need of loving homes

2. How AWESOME these kids were

Adoption made sense and because it was right for my husband and I, I wrongly put the expectation on others that they TOO should feel called to take in children that needed loving families.

My advocacy was rooted in judgement and ignorance. I know that now. Life is a powerful teacher and yet, God used my broken thinking to help others see beauty in opening their homes to non-biological children. Perhaps, that wouldn't have been the case, if not for my big, bold mouth having been wide open! (Ugh... really, Brooke?!)

I'll never forget a conversation with one of my dearest friends that took place shortly after she and her husband had decided to adopt from overseas. They were in the process of being matched with their adoptive child. In the waiting, they were eager to learn from us all they could soak up about our experience as adoptive parents. You see, at the time we had 5 children. Three of our kids were special needs babies that had grown into the happiest, sweetest preschoolers you could imagine. The other two were hot-headed teens that were dead-set on hurting Jason and I in order that they wouldn't be the only ones hurting in our home. We didn't fully understand the dynamics the way we do as we can look backwards now. We did, however, know that older children with histories of neglect, abuse, or abandonment that came into our home were exponentially more difficult than those that came to us directly after discharge from the hospital as babies. We knew this not just based on the licensing trainings, but now we knew it first hand as we lived daily in the struggles of trying to neutralize our home. Our previously stable home was now chronically hot or cold based on the ways in which our oldest children would wake up. This family embarking on their first adoption journey knew a lot about what we were experiencing and would seek understanding as to how it would apply to their lives as soon-to-be adoptive parents.

Anyway, my girlfriend had gotten up off the couch where we had conversations about adoption that had already lasted hours. She was a bit frustrated about the direction our talk had gone that evening and had left to create a bit of distance for processing and to get a drink from the kitchen. Upon her return she stated, "My son is not broken and I don't like the way you keep talking to me like he is." I was taken back at first because it felt like I had inadvertently offended my dearest friend and her protective Mama Bear had reared her head.

I don't remember what I replied at the time and can only hope it was both compassionate and tender. I do know, however, that her son was broken then, regardless of which boy she would have soon been matched to. Not one orphan kept overseas is without a tremendous amount of loss, grief, fear, pain, and confusion. Not one child that has lost their parent for any reason, regardless of location, is "whole". God's design for family is clearly stated in scripture as a woman leaving her family and a man doing the same in order to be married and one flesh. In that oneness, they are to bear children and raise them in the "ways in which they shall go so that they will not depart from it". Every child deserves to be raised by their biological mother and father in a perfect world.

The good news is, by thinking about the brokenness of an adopted child, we could either apply that across the board (in which case, are all broken as humans), or we should wipe the slate clean for both those kids and the rest of humankind. Is there one person you know that hasn't gone through things that have left them battle scarred and worn? Is there one person that you can think of that has lived any length of life and hasn't experienced loss, pain, isolation, judgement, or injustice? We all have and all will. And just as though it is nobody's job to "fix" that brokenness that lies inside you and I, it is not anyone's job to look for the brokenness in the heart, mind, and soul of an adopted child and simply "fix" it.

Adoption isn't for the purpose of "righting the wrongs" in the life of a child. Adoption isn't to "fix" the hurt within an adoptive child. Adoption is a chance to take a child worthy of love, family, and a chance to reach their highest potential and place them into a loving adoptive home in order that they get a chance to find themselves fully despite their pains and fears.

As a mother, when a small child falls and scrapes their knee they turn to me. I am their comforter. I am the one that cleans the wound, protects it with a bandage, and prays over the little one for healing and peace. A child doesn't turn within themselves to solve their need in their pain. A child doesn't turn to Jesus to be the answer for their hurt. A child turns to a mother to meet the tangible needs that are imminent. And as a mother, I am wired to meet these needs. I run to my child to ensure they see that they are valued and that I am concerned. I show my care as I apply the remedies for their wound and pains and my child learns that I can be trusted to show up in a time of hurt.

Often times, as adopted children struggle more and more with identity, grief, social connections, academics, and more, adoptive mothers can want to be the solution to the many complex differences within their adoptive children. Moms can find themselves in fear and grief and want more than anything to "heal" their children from their afflictions as they seemingly did when their child was a baby. Logically, we moms know we cannot heal our children. We can only love them, provide tools, skills, and resources fort them, and let our kids find the solutions within themselves and with these supports as they age into maturity. We can do the best we can to protect them from others and themselves, until they are of an age where we no longer need to be that coach.

The fact that adoptive moms can't "fix" what is going on in their adoptive children is actually a blessing in disguise. When moms work hard to be the healer, protector, lover, peace-maker, chef, house keeper, mediator, etc for their children they do not learn to look within themselves and their relationship with the Lord for solutions to their hurts and voids. Despite the truth that adoptive parents can never fix these "holes", it can leave adoptive parents feeling like failures and feeling horribly ill-equipped for the task of raising their adopted child.

HOW CAN YOU HELP?

1. Are you ready to accept that the grief and loss is real for EVERY adopted child? Even children placed at birth directly into their adoptive homes have adoption trauma and are likely to have differences as they grow into adulthood (no matter how precious and happy they are as babies). If you want more information on the impact of adoption on newborns I would recommend reading "Primal Wound" by Nancy Verrier.

2. Once you recognize that adoption trauma and any neglect, abuse, or abandonment prior to being placed in the child's adoptive home leads to a "brokenness", can you accept that in light of this, the child will likely have fear, anger, and grief based behaviors at stages of childhood and adolescence? Can you work to find acceptance of this rather than judgement toward the child for the ways in which their immature bodies and brains process their stories?

3. Can you lead with compassion for the adopted child, knowing that the child had no choice in losing their birth family and no choice in where they would end up? Can you have compassion toward the adoptive parents for the facts that they simply cannot heal wounds they didn't create, and they are not responsible to "fix" their adopted children?

4. Can you choose to see everything that looks like "failure" is an opportunity for the parents and the child to turn to the Lord and to turn within themselves for solutions to the hurtful or difficult situation? Even adoptive parents need to be refined and must press into the Lord for solutions to the issues within their homes (,) rather than expecting the child to "get better" so everything else can be better.

CHAPTER 2

YES, WE ARE ALL VERY REAL.

Forgive me if as you are reading this seems all too obvious. I know for me, the first time I was asked if "these were my 'real 'children", I was definitely confused by the choice of words. At first I thought the question was a fluke. Time proved quickly that when people in the world see adoptive families with different ethnicities, in an attempt to reconcile the relationship dynamics in their own heads, silly questions tend to come out! (It's unfair that everywhere our family goes, because of our different ethnicities, we are seen as an adoptive family. It's unfair that my children can't go out in our community and stand beside parents and siblings without an automatic level of "adopted".)

When we had three children ranging only 18 months in age, and made up of 2 different ethnicities, we would get head tilts followed by inquisitive eyes. We could tangibly see the wheels turning in the onlooker's head and then things inevitably come out like:

"Are they…. um…. twins?"

"Are these your real kids?"

"Are they actual siblings?"

"Are you keeping them?"

Though the questions seem relatively harmless and simply rooted in a lack of understanding, let's just put yourself in the shoes of the child as these questions are being asked year after year as the children grow up with parents and siblings of varying ethnic and life backgrounds?

If you think back to when you were an adolescent, you may remember just wanting to fit in with your peers. Fitting in by dressing how your friends did, styling hair like others, even picking up the slang terms and owning the same toys likely helped you to avoid judgements, criticisms, or bullying. Early on, children learn that differences lead to misunderstandings, over which some other children act out in simply cruel ways. In order to avoid painful glances, underhanded giggles between classmates, mean comments about unique freckles or off-brand shoes, children will try hard to blend in. Now let's revisit the comments from onlookers as these adopted children go out with their adoptive families...

"Are they... twins?" "Are they actual siblings?" The question of "actual siblings" is intended to state "biological siblings" but the correct terminology isn't there for the onlooker to draw from. And clearly, my children are not twins. They are close in age but not even remotely close in ethnic traits. Skin, hair, facial features, and even size are and have always been drastically different between the children in question. And though a simple "no, they are just beautiful siblings" is a sufficient answer between the adults having the conversation, the child hears "I don't understand why your kids are so different than other siblings". A child already insecure around identity and belonging is now frequently reminded that they are not tied to their adoptive family in a way in which the family unit doesn't come under question. The child has to face the inquisitive looks, the perplexed questions, and even watch their parents defend the beauty of the unique make-up of the family that the adoptive child didn't get any say over joining.

"Are these your real kids?" is a question that upsets many adoptive families. The children are VERY real. The adoptive parents are VERY real. Nothing about an adoptive family isn't real and yet again, the question is simply mis-stated due to a lack of information to draw from. The onlooker is intending to ask "are these your biological children?" And though the answer to this question is really not something that strangers or casual contacts should be privy to, it doesn't prevent the awkward situation of being asked in front of the children.

When a child is asked if they are their adoptive parents ' real kids, they can interpret this as being an outsider to the family. The child can be reminded of the grief they have from losing the mother that likely they looked much more similar to them. The child can feel as though they don't fit in and that the color of their skin or their unique physical differences that require explanations for differences that most kids done ever even have to consider. Adopted children that don't look like their adoptive parents are always desperately trying to blend in so the world won't notice the differences.

Adopted children are adopted because they were not able to be raised by their birth mom. This means a birth mom gave them to an adoptive family OR they were taken from a birth mom for reasons of neglect, abuse, or abandonment. When a child is seen as adopted, often they feel like they are seen as either "given away" or "raised by a bad mom" as they get into adolescent years. This happens sometimes even if they were much younger and were previously proud to be adopted and loved their identity as adopted. Bringing up these negative thoughts or labels for a child struggling with confidence, identity, reconciling their past, or processing hard things in therapy is not helpful and easily avoided.

How You Can Help?

1. Do you need to know the story of how a family came to be (,) if you are not already close enough to the family to have been told? Just because a person is curious about other people doesn't entitle them to the answers. Allowing an adoptive or foster family to just be seen as "a family" can be a tremendous gift to the children.

2. Is there opportunity to ask the questions you have regarding a family and their adoption status when the children are not around? Because you don't know the view or histories of the children involved, waiting to ask questions in an adult to adult conversation protects the children from questions that may bring up negative feelings for them.

3. Recognize that the sibling relationships within an adoptive home are their new, permanent family relationships. They are trying to connect with siblings that also have complexities and childhood differences. Pointing out differences to adopted siblings by asking if they are "real siblings" only adds to difficulties in attaching and accepting the new sibling relationships.

CHAPTER 3

FAMILY LEGACY STILL EXISTS

Legal Ties May or May Not Exist

As mentioned, Jason and I have 11 children that we are the parents to... boys and girls. Some are legally adopted and others are not, which is no fault of theirs or ours. Adoption is a legal process before the courts in the United States for most people. For us, adoption is a decision to be a mother and father for a child we are called to. In our family, adoption isn't a legal process. A formal court adoption in our family represents the legal affirming of a decision made long before any court date or finalization by a court. We have children that are not able to be legally adopted for a multitude of reasons, however, we are still fully "Mom" and "Dad" to them regardless of any court given authority. This can be difficult for the world to understand... which I can see. And yet we do not need society to align with our view as it is a decision between us and the Lord and our children. Because of the calling in our lives for each one of our children in every capacity, we show up for these "adopted" children just the same as we would if adoption papers existed for these relationships.

Why do I start a section on "family legacy" with the aforementioned? Well, I am so glad you asked. It is important that every adopted family be given the freedom to define themselves as they feel is appropriate. I know an adoptive family that brought in a child from another country that was "listed" as an only child when they brought her home. Their new adoptive child was home for over a year before the adoptive family learned that there was a biological sibling to their newly adopted child back in the home country of this child. Their new daughter was struck with fear and grief about the sibling that they hadn't seen in many, many years. This family believed that getting on a plane to locate the biological sibling to their new adoptive daughter was necessary for their daughter to have closure and the necessary information to embrace her new life. As you can imagine, this journey changed the family forever. The sibling was alive and struggling with extreme poverty. The located sibling was, from the day of discovery onward, accepted as a new child and dependent to the parents in the adoptive home regardless of what the courts would decide about the ability for this child to travel back overseas to join this family physically.

Adoptive families have children with a history outside the adoptive parents. It is because of this history that adoptive parents may need to make decisions about familial roles that go outside of what would be considered typical or normal. And because extended family can't understand the decision, or the decisions aren't legal decisions, often these "bonus children" get treated different than the other members of the family of similar age and "relationship status". Let's visit this point deeper.

Imagine you are a child that has already endured one of the greatest pains known to mankind, the loss of your biological mother whether simply because the government "saved" you from the extreme abuse within that relationship, or because your mother grew ill and died before your eyes.

You don't know who will take care of you. You aren't sure if you will have a mom to turn to on holidays and to discuss the hardest moments of your life that certainly lie ahead. Then one day, the Lord opens a door by establishing a relationship with someone who is willing to help you by meeting some of your basic needs. Not only do basic needs get met, but they speak to you about perhaps joining your family and getting a chance to stay in one stable place with love, educational opportunities, an abundance of food and clothing... possibly with a biological sibling, as in the case of my friend's story. So many answered prayers just in the *hope* of a future with this family. That hope and the conversations with this new "mom and dad" are the very things that allow you to sleep with some peace at night.

Now stay in that mindset, but instead of the courts allowing your placement within the family to occur, the courts instead keep you stuck where you are because the abuse isn't "bad enough" to be removed. Or instead of coming into this family, the embassy on the other side of the planet denies your visa for unknown reasons time after time after time. All the while, your hope is challenged but your "new mom and dad" are trying to assure you that there must be another way. Time keeps ticking, strategies change as new plans are tried. The question becomes, if the courts don't get on board, do we then sever the relationship and all the hope within it? Over these years the child in need of family has grown to love the "parents" and the "parents" have sacrificed for this child in time, money, prayer, and emotion for years in ways that have put their love and commitment on full display to the child that is caught in the fails of the system. Should the parents simply stop loving this hurting, afraid child because the courts haven't caught up to what God has already done in the relationship? Would you be able to love and give within a relationship for years and walk away, crushing the child, simply because the "yes" didn't come in ideal timing or paperwork wasn't finalized? Or simply because the child is growing up into a young adult? How would you decide when to walk away? How would you explain to a child, now several years older, that you have loved them (not just lip service but you sacrificed and worked to bring this child home so you clearly loved them) but now with no paperwork or with finalization issues, that you no longer will hold that same relational place in your heart for them due to no fault of their own? Can you see why adoptive parents sometimes have "children" they are not legally tied to but that they choose to add to their family photos, will, and child count? These children become a part of a complex family legacy.

Legacy Despite Genetics

Jason and I learned that we would not be having biological children and that adoption was going to be the way in which God would grow our family, and when this became the reality for both my parents and his parents, there was some layer of grief on both my husband's side and my side of our extended family. Interestingly enough, Jason and I both have one biological sibling and neither of them had children of their own as our family continued to expand. It became apparent at a point in time that there would be no biological child on either side to carry forward the blood line with the family names. I hadn't considered that this would be a loss for my parents or Jason's. We had kids. In every sense of the word, I considered them an offspring in our family the same way as I would a biological child. These children would be the ones to carry forward the torch from generation to generation and why that needed to be yoked to bloodline didn't make sense to me. And yet, that also brought up some honest grief that I would need to process as well.

I would never know what it was like to look into "my" child's eyes and see the eyes that I saw looking back at me in my own baby photos. I would never be able to see the Lord's perfect blend between my physical features and my husband's. When in a parent teacher conference, I would not be able to lean over to my spouse and tell him how our son or daughter got all of their brains from him. To me, at the end of the day these things were a small thing to have to let go of. Yet if you look at any social media outlet, you will see parents proudly posting baby pictures asking others to chime in with opinions on who New Baby most closely resembles, mom or dad. Parents enjoy watching how God blends the beauty of adults into the attributes of offspring. Missing out on this is a part meant grief and acceptance for us adoptive parents and grandparents alike.

One of the things that I longed for far more than seeing my eyes or cheeks in the face of my children was the pregnancy experience. Many women love pregnancy... and many women hate being pregnant. Yet nearly all women that have biological children can agree that hearing a heartbeat from within their own womb was an experience that they would never take back. The miracle of a life within a life is simply priceless. Now that I am a grandmother and I get to go to ultrasound appointments for many of my grandkids, I can say that I knew I had missed out by not getting to see the fuzzy impressions of a baby not yet fully physically formed but it is far greater than I even knew. I longed to feel the kicks and flutters of movement from within my flesh. I longed to sing to a baby within my tummy and rub my tummy while praying over my son or daughter every night and all day, every day. I had to have space and permission to grieve what wasn't, not just be in acceptance for our path of adoption that lied ahead.

HOW CAN YOU HELP?

1. If your family member chooses to love a child as if he/she is their own, with all the blessings and burdens of taking on this role, are you willing to be accepting of their decision despite whether you agree or disagree with the decision?

2. Will you define your role with a non-legally adopted child in your family based on the parents' assignment of the role or the court's/government's assignment of their role? Is this a space where you are willing to have a discussion with the adoptive family centered on a common understanding of what each of you would ideally like this relationship to look like?

3. Do you have thoughts of grief around what you will "miss out on" if the adoptive family that is in your biological family never has a child to you genetically? Is that grief something you can work on personally without making your grief an issue for the adoptive family to need to "solve"?

4. What "benefits" of family legacy would a biological child receive that was born into your family? Do you feel differently about allowing those benefits to an adoptive child instead? Why and how can you communicate any differences in a way that doesn't seem punitive to the adoptive family for their decision to adopt? How can you communicate any differences in a way that doesn't further cause an adoptive child to feel like they lost their birth family and now are not fully accepted in their adoptive family?

5. Do you see signs that the adoptive family in your life is grieving a loss of the things that a biological child would provide in their parenting journey that an adoptive child cannot (like the pregnancy experience or common attributes to the parents)? Are you sensitive to the fact that adoption and loss go together like peas and carrots? The child loses a genetic tie to their birth family along with their own genetic identity and the adoptive parents lose out on things much less significant than those of the child, yet still very real. Are you compassionate for the losses and complexities without the inconvenience of these realities causing you to feel as though it is just too much and thus pass a judgement that adoption isn't right for your loved ones?

6. How will the rights of inheritance be established within your family, knowing that parts of your family are not genetically connected to you? Once you have reconciled those thoughts and that decision, can you communicate that decision to the adoptive parents in order that they will know how you feel while you are still here to be able to have that discussion?

CHAPTER 4

WHEN PRAISING ADOPTIVE PARENTS CREATES PAIN

This may be one of the harder points of supporting an adoptive family to write about. As you can imagine, most of us adoptive mamas are pretty compassionate and really try to take care of everyone's feelings within relationships. Many people in my world will read this. As they read this, they may feel uncertain about things they have said in the past. You may be reading this book because an adoptive family has shared it with you, and you may feel uncertain about things you have said in your past. So let me start by saying this… It is because people love us that people will want to encourage and support us as adoptive parents. Our friends will hear about our hurts or recognize the neurodiversity of our children and then want to shout out how much they admire the ways in which we show up for our adoptive children. The intentions of those praising Jason and I for all we do to lead our family toward Christ and shepherd our children through their own difficulties are received as nothing but loving by us as parents.

Jason and I make a little joke that we don't "go" places, "we descend upon them". There are so many reasons that when our family is out in society that we get noticed. We have a large family with a very wide age range. We have a diverse family that cannot be missed. We have every shade of brown within the skin colors in our home. We have a few kids (ok and perhaps I am no exception) that are on the louder side while others try to disappear into thin air as we make a playful scene around us. We go out to eat or to our 9am church service and we are used to being seen and it is usually in a very friendly and engaging way. Because people cannot fathom adopting eleven children, it can be seen as admirable and evidence of our love not just for our children, but for our calling in our faith walk with Jesus. When people see things as "extraordinary", they tend to compliment the parent that is doing the "extraordinary" thing.

If Jason and I were curing cancer, praising us wouldn't create any secondary concerns. If Jason and I were incredible artists, again, the praise is only to the glory of God without a cost toward anyone else. Even when Jason and I are overseas serving the Lord by loving the orphans and impoverished within Ethiopia, the praise is given and the children we touch for the 2 weeks while we are there, would simply join in the praise if they were actually in the audience at the time the praise was given. So why is this any different?

Let's say that my daughter is with us at the time that someone approaches Jason and I in a church foyer. We are standing around chatting when a gentleman comes up to us and shakes our hands. He goes on to say, "I heard you have adopted eleven kids?! That is spectacular. I don't know how you do that because I could never adopt. But I just wanted to shake your hand and tell you I admire what you are doing." It seems inconspicuous enough, right? Let me tell you, over the last 20 years as an adoptive family, this EXACT conversation has happened hundreds of times, both privately and very publicly with my children listening in.

What do my adopted children hear? Let's assume for a second that the adoptive children between the ages of 10-20 years old are starting to question why they had to be adopted in the first place. These are those years of development that the complex reasoning kicks in and the children tend to start internalizing their own script and understanding about who they are and why they were adopted. Let's assume that in light of this, my children are feeling a little like "a baby thrown out with the bath water". Let's also assume that my children are old enough to recognize that they had *reasons* that they had to be removed from biological family members and placed into our adoptive home, and that those reasons create a lens of embarrassment and shame for them at this stage of development in their lives. No one wants to be defined by in utero exposures or past abuses. Lastly, let's assume that my children are struggling socially as most adopted children do by the ages of 10-20 and that being "normal" in front of their peers is the thing they want most when it comes to how others see them.

Now that you know more about the mindset and heart of the children listening into the above conversation, let's write down ways in which one of our adoptees may interpret the compliments given to us as parents:

"My parents are so amazing for raising their child? I don't get it. They chose us and raising their kids is just what parents are supposed to do. This doesn't make sense."

"Right... so no different than the programs that sponsor sections of the highway to clean up the trash, my parents have 'taken in the unwanted trash that was thrown to the side ' and now they are amazing because my value is so low that others would never do that."

"Great. Now others know that I have something wrong with me or a history with another family. I had so hoped they thought humans were like cats and could have a "mixed color litter" because I just don't want to have to answer these questions with people who are more curious about my past and pain than they are about who I am today."

"My parents actually aren't as great as ya'll think they are. They don't understand me. I wish I wasn't adopted into this family but if I wasn't, where would I go? My dad tells the dumbest jokes and my mom is so controlling. I wish they knew how things really were because if they did, they would see that I am not the problem that I have been labeled."

Children want to be seen as normal and for who they are, not how they came into a family- period. Young adoptees may be proud to be adopted when they are 6 but rarely still brag about it by age 12.

As adults, we can recognize the sacrifices that are made out of love and commitment to our adopted children in our homes. Society can see that when a family brings in adopted children, they are choosing to bring in a child with a ton of pain and grief. Culturally, most know that adopted children have higher needs in school, in mental health, and in supports within the family home. It is for these reasons that the parents are praised for their commitment to adoption and yet the praises of these parents **in front of adoptive children** can reinforce internal messages rooted in shame. It tells them unintentionally that they have less value than a biological child in a biological family does and that these adopted children are burdensome in their position within their family. Can you see how the adoptee can interpret the innocuous praises of their parents in such harmful ways?

So if this is true (which it is), why have Jason and I allowed it? The answer to this question is complicated in that without telling the beauty of adoption, how do people know the beauty? And if people cannot see the beauty of adoption for what it is, how will they feel compelled to open up their homes and hearts to children whom desperately need families to call them theirs? To my knowledge, the testimony of our family has resulted in over 50 children being placed in loving homes. God is using our pains, struggles, joys and victories to further the good work in families all across the United States. And yet, what is the cost? Jason and I have several teen/young adults at home right now. Every one of them has a more extreme form of self-esteem struggle than the average teen in our culture (which is already high post Covid). All three of our teen/young adult children are socially anxious and struggle to find their voice in communicating. The continued messages from well-meaning onlookers hasn't created these issues, but is no doubt a part of what exacerbates it.

What can be said instead?

"What a beautiful family! We really love watching God knit together the best of his children all into one home!"

"Isn't a cool thing to walk in adoption as ALL OF US are adopted into God's family?! Your family is a great depiction of this."

"The way your family comes together to navigate the roller coasters of life is truly beautiful. We are blessed to be your cheerleaders."

A slight shift of the things said in front of adopted children can help them feel seen, valued, and yet "less broken". Small shifts in language can help adoptees still grieving "what could have been" in their bio families not feel more wounded and resentful of the path they were forced on instead of the path they were born into with their biological parents.

HOW CAN YOU HELP?

1. When adoptive parents turn praises put onto them back onto their children, take that as a cue that what was said may have been a statement hard for both the parents and the children to hear. This is a common way adoptive parents tend to try to rebalance the statement to be more palatable to the adoptive family. (Example: "That's amazing that you guys adopted all these kids" would then be deflected to "It's our kids that are amazing, not us".

2. Don't be afraid to speak up! The last things adoptive families want is to be "normalized" and not have a platform for others to be open to the idea of fostering or adopting within their own homes. Just choose when and how you speak up so that it can be done in ways that honor the children and respect their privacy as much as possible.

3. When the children are around and you want to address the parents in their role as adoptive parents, make sure whatever you say affirms value to the children, not just the parents. If you really prayerfully seek understanding about the heart of the orphan that leads them to be in a position of needing adoption, compassion will fall on you. As you are touched by the compassion for these children, remember to use that compassion not just for all the adoptive parents are doing in an attempt to be the best parents they can be for their family, but for the kids who are enduring more

than any child should have to as they navigate an adolescence without their biological parents.

4. Leave any desire to have conversations about the pains, difficulties, and commitments of adoptive parents to be had when the adoptive parents are alone and away from their children (biological and adopted children). Some adoptive parents may be in a season where they are less open to sharing. Others are open books in the hopes that others will want to join in the adoption movement. Regardless, respect that each adoptive parent and child has a story that is theirs alone. Anything shared with you should be assumed as confidential and not a cause for "shock and awe" stories within social circles.

Chapter 5

The Story Is Still Unwritten... Non-Disclosure Agreements

Do you know what an NDA (Non-Disclosure Agreement) is? When a company has a new technology or invention coming to market but needs to test the product, anyone given early access to the proprietary information is asked to sign an NDA. By signing this legal document, the secret information revealed to the product tester cannot be stollen for personal gain or given to a competitor in order that the product can come to market by anyone other than the original inventor. This NDA protects the company that has already invested time and money into the product so that their investment has the opportunity to return profits. This is exactly what insider access to an adoptive family is like. Though it is highly unlikely that any adoptive parents or adoptive kiddos will ask you to sign an NDA, I would like to ask you that as a part of the support system, you would consider any receiving of confidential, private information an automatic signature on an NDA for the family and members within it.

Do you remember doing something really wrong as a child? Do you remember a parent or older sibling telling others right in front of you the awful thing you had done? It is humiliating, embarrassing, and can be very wounding. Adoptive children tend to have shame about where they come from and any drug exposure, abuse, or abandonment that came prior to their adoptions. Often embarrassed kids mask pretending not to be ashamed, present with false arrogance/indifference about it, or withdrawal from others falling alone into their shame.

Many adopted children in the US have a biological family with addiction and/or mental illness. This is something that no child would be proud of. Many adoptees in the US were exposed to drugs or alcohol in the womb. Others were severely neglected or abused after birth. Children from overseas often have painful memories of losing their biological mother and terrors from their time being institutionalized. No matter the child's story, it isn't a story wrapped up in pretty paper and adorned with ribbons.

A common misunderstanding within the less experienced adoptive community is that when a child is brought out of trauma and a chaotic/unhealthy environment and placed into a stable, loving, nurturing home the home will become the emotionally influential force on the child. Statistically speaking, this couldn't be more false. A child with internal trauma wounds from their past cannot simply change their trauma responses because of an environmental change (we will address this more later). In light of this, a once stable home tends to become more chaotic when infused with the maladaptive behaviors of trauma-exposed kids. This is important to understand because behaviors WILL come when an adopted child enters the adoptive family. This is expected. This is normal. And this can be very ugly, depending on the circumstances.

An adopted child can struggle to accept their new home, process their hurts and fears, and wrestle with identity over their present and past. In that, maladaptive behaviors can show up and the child can be labeled as "bad". And yet, if I as a grown adult, were to lose the person closest to me in my adult life, then have to uproot and move, take on new roommates and the roommates were to decide what my access and rules in my new communal home were, is there any scenario in which I, as an adult, would just slide in without a lot of intense emotions and more extreme behaviors than anyone would expect from me? Of course not. My grief, fear, confusion, and pain would cause my hardest season in life to show up in unknown ways.

Children are just that- children. They don't have maturity. They don't have life experience like an adult does. They don't have good complex reasoning skills. They lack impulse control, the ability to predict consequences, and internal motivation. I just described ALL children. Now take that normal child and pour a TREMENDOUS amount of grief, loss, fear, confusion, social differences, dysfunctional exposures, and medical differences onto them. What do you think is the expected presentation of THAT child? Yet teachers, adoptive grandparents, sometimes adoptive parents, and certainly a good portion of service providers for these children expect that the child will be resilient and easily overcome the difficulties with just love and a stable environment. That is rarely the case, which isn't easy, but is expected.

When an adopted child has maladaptive behaviors, it can be off-putting for the adoptive parents or those caring for the adopted child. In my world as a Children's Director at my church and in my career providing trauma informed care, I see some things over and over again:

"Excuse my grandson. He as adopted and his birth mom did drugs. Her boyfriend would go on benders and come home and beat them both up so he is more violent than most kids and has an inability to sit in his seat."

"I am so frustrated. My children decided to adopt and now my grandkids are all unruly disasters because their old mom didn't take care of them."

"I will not tolerate my daughter's 16 year old. She is a horrible kid and is so disrespectful. I think her mom used to give her drugs and it messed her up. So now she is defiant, lazy, and out of control. My children aren't doing anything about it and I have written her out of our will. I am not going to be the one that tolerates her behaviors."

Regardless of the cause, people tend to overshare in order that the poor behaviors are understood or justified. Parents, grandparents, and others are embarrassed by the misconduct of trauma kids. They don't want the poor behaviors wrongly assigned as being "caused" by the new adoptive family or themselves. It's as if to say "I don't condone the behaviors but please don't think it is because I am a bad parent/grandparent." Why is the image of the adoptive family (or other person from the examples) more important than preventing added shame and judgement for the struggling child? It shouldn't be.

What kinds of things can you say instead?

"This is my grandson. He seems to be having a bit of a hard day. Please let me know if you need my added support."

"This student has some neuro differences. The things that have helped him to do his best are _____, _____, and _____."

"Please pray for our family as our adopted grandson finds his 'walking legs'. We are so proud of him for continuing to show up and yet we have a ways to go before he is able to reach his highest potential. The journey is hard but one we are excited to come out of it singing the praises of God for full healing."

Many of my adopted teens were REALLY hard to raise and live with. They had a lot of justified reasons to act out. They had a lot of reasons to build up walls between themselves and us parents. They had reasons to hate themselves, others, and life in general. None of that excuses the ways in which they processed their feelings that hurt us parents or the other members of the family, and yet, their stories were still unwritten. Today, I confidently look at my adult children with pride for the adults they have chosen to become. Had we stopped believing in them, had we stopped loving them in their ugliness, had we given up the long and painful fight, I truly believe they would not be where they are today. Many of my children are the first in their biological family to have graduated high school, the first to graduate college, the first to not be imprisoned by age 18, the first to own a home and the first to own their own successful businesses. Was it hard? Was it ugly? Yes it was at times. Was it worth it and am I glad that I allowed the story to still unfold? Absolutely YES to both.

HOW CAN YOU HELP?

1. When adopted children show up with unhealthy attitudes and behaviors, work hard to remember that they are still a child. The human brain is not fully matured until age 25. Regardless of the behaviors you see, remember that they are young and have real trauma wounds that drive their unhelpful, unhealthy ways of doing life and relationships RIGHT NOW. That doesn't mean it will always be that way.

2. Are you a source of support or added shame? Children that are feeling unsuccessful in their adoptive home

do not benefit from more rejection by others in their lives. Conversations starting with "what is wrong with you" or that point out what "normal" kids their age are doing only add to the child's shame which typically creates more unhealthy behaviors over the course of the long run despite a perhaps short term, temporary correction in behavior.

3. When you see the adoptive parents struggling, do you want to end the book and cancel the story? Adoptive parents will fall into doubt on dark days when the pain in front of their nose is greater than their ability to see the current situation as a chapter. Scripture says that in a timeline, our whole human life is as short as a vapor. The season of pain in raising a hurting adopted child is a fraction of a vapor. If you want to be helpful, allow the adoptive parent to share their fear and hurts. Then remind those parents that the story is still unwritten and that you are a support regardless of where this book is headed.

4. You don't need to explain yourself or the behaviors of the adoptee. I understand that an unruly child can be embarrassing and the ability to explain away the hitting, cursing, or disrespect makes it feel less personal to you. Just remember that in doing so, you have put a label on your adoptee that cannot be unheard and could spread throughout your community. If your child is 5 today when you disclose the horrors of his past, how will he feel about those he knows having his private story when he is 15 and in the peak of puberty? Will his prior sexual trauma, his prior drug exposure, or his birth mom previously starving him help him with shame and attachment or hurt him? Will other parents of his peers worry about his

influence on their kids when he is older? How will your son feel about all the people in his circle knowing his "case file" and could it be used against him by peers or acquaintances if the information got into the wrong hands?

Chapter 6

Do You Really Know The Adopted Child?

The Honeymoon

So many of my children came into our home "determined" to succeed. Most had faced loss not just once... they had faced loss over and over. These kids were masters of resilience and had put on their best selves in order to make our family work out for them. Some of them thought our family lifestyle was of "the rich and famous" simply because they could have more than one pair of shoes and not buy their only clothes from Walmart. Others thought our home was simply a stepping stone in which they would not "need" anything from us. Instead, these kids would tolerate us in order to get what they wanted for themselves, or to achieve independence and their own life goals outside of family or relationship (because having parents hurt too much so it was easier to pretend they weren't wanted or needed). No matter what the thinking was as a child came into our family, each child was determined to not have to reinsert themselves into yet another family and start over. They didn't want to "fail" or be "rejected". Either idea was crippling whether conscious or subconscious. This is why most kids come to us as people-pleasers in the beginning. We name this phase the "honeymoon". This period can last hours, days, weeks, or months but is certainly going to come to an end as the child feels either more secure in the relationships within the home OR gives up on trying to be perfect and sabotages. Sabotage would look like massive attempts to reject the family on their terms rather than face a possible rejection from the parents. If you are meeting a child during their honeymoon phase, you do not know the secure version of this child. You likely know the adjusting version of this child which will obviously be quite appealing, in most cases.

Superficial Attachment

Superficial attachment from trauma children is a common maladaptive presentation. Affection and emotional intimacy in relationship generally take time with children that are bonded to their biological parents. Children whom get their needs met by a stable, healthy source such as a biological mom don't need a stranger or acquaintance for anything in their lives. Because the needs are met, the child can choose more carefully who to insert into their inner circle. Trauma kids, on the other hand, don't understand healthy attachment. Trauma kids don't have one consistent source to go to for their emotional, physical, or spiritual needs to be met as biological children with a stable mom figure does. It is for this reason that trauma kids sometimes will become extra snuggly, extra sweet, extra "cute" with people that are NOT their adoptive parents. Adoptive parents require relationship and have boundaries and expectations. Relationship and expectations can be very difficult for trauma kids to navigate. So, unless the child is still in the honeymoon period, trauma kids will often withhold the snuggly, cute, sweet version of themselves from the adoptive parents (unless looking for something manipulatively) and instead pour it into the acquaintances or distant relatives of the adoptive family. The child resists the work of attachment with the parental figures and meets physical and emotional needs in a way that feels better in the moment but that is ultimately a stumbling block to their healthy growth and long term needs and development.

Control

Control is one of the greatest wants for all children, but exponentially so for trauma kids. When control was given to (or required by) a parental figure in their lives before adoption, it led to a tremendous amount of pain and grief. In light of these hurts, trauma kids with (will?) fight hard to get and maintain control of most everything in their lives. This is typically done through fight, flight, freeze or faun behaviors. Fight behaviors push away people that are creating discomfort through expectations, boundaries, or even abuses. Flight behaviors remove themselves from discomfort created by those same expectations, boundaries, or abuses. Freeze behaviors are an internal flight response in which the child doesn't move, speak or both but shuts down in the face of those same discomforts. Faun behaviors are superficial attachment, snuggles, and puppy dog eyes designed to steal hearts in order to get needs met.

For people in the lives of our trauma kids, these needs for control can show up in 2 ways. The first way is that the acquaintances in the life of the child don't have very big expectations or boundaries and are seen as non-abusive. This means that the child doesn't have cause to show up with their control behaviors to the same extent that they do at home. A lack of intimate, normal relationship requirement is often enough for the child to be more "pleasant" in their conduct than they would be with their parents. The child may get the "fun" parts of relationship like ice cream trips with grandma or thrift store shopping with an aunt but not have to comply with tech rules or eating their veggies. The child may show up stable and sweet in the face of these kinds of circumstances.

When the acquaintance or family member tries to enforce an expectation or boundary, or raises their voice and seems 'abusive', the child falls into fight, flight, freeze or faun behaviors. The child may withhold communication and pout despite their age. The child may throw a tantrum equivalent to a toddler. The child may even try to run out the door. The child may knock a framed picture off the wall "accidentally" or lash out with hateful language. The child may pull out the best snuggles and pleading eyes. Switching back and forth between the strategies is also highly likely.

The second way trauma kids 'need for control shows up is through demanding the control directly through words and actions. Trauma kids can demand or ask for what they went and then "punish" the people in their lives when they don't get what they want. This can look like emotional extortion, withholding communication and appropriate engagement. It can also look like name calling, stomping, yelling, or other direct rebellions against the lack of control.

Manipulation

How does a child get a second piece of Easter candy when Mom says no more? How do kids get the greeter at a store to go find them a sticker as they exit? How do kids get Dad to buy them a Hot Wheel from the toy aisle on a grocery run? All children starting at a really young age learn how to whine, put on "puppy dog eyes" and justify getting what they want in the form of manipulation. But how does a hungry child get fed when they can't turn to the parents in their lives? How does a child get new shoes when they have outgrown their old ones and their parents have no money for shoes? How does a child get turned free when caught stealing from the convenience store rather than the cops getting called?

Manipulation becomes a part of survival for kids that are abused, neglected, or abandoned after birth. It isn't a skill used to get what they want. It is a skill refined and perfected in many cases to get what they need. When kids are young, cute, and in desperate circumstances manipulation is highly effective. Have you been to a third world country such as Ethiopia? Or non-tourist parts of Mexico? Have you seen the children with no shoes and fungal infection on their skin? Children with tissue-paper thin clothing that has weeks ' worth of dirt on it? When they reach out their hands and stare up at you with their big ol 'eyes, it is very hard not to put something in that bare palm. The manipulations are effective and they work. Because they work, they repeat the behaviors.

When a child has had to manipulate others to get their needs met, letting go of the manipulations without a lot of time, instruction, and discipline is an unrealistic expectation. The problem, of course, is that often times the prey are not aware of the manipulations when they don't come from a street child with their hands out. In the case of a third world country, we know exactly what is happening and we willingly choose to either give to the child or not. In the case of an adoptive child, the manipulations are often masked as truths but serve a hidden agenda.

We had a child come to us as a tween. This child told us that the birth family made them choose a scary movie at the discount theater for their birthday. This child went on to tell us how awful it was to go to a horror movie because of the terror in their life and how much they hated horror films. We were sympathetic and appalled! What kind of guardian would do that to a child on their birthday?!! Within 2 months, we saw this same child wanting to watch horror films when renting movies was an option (which we were NOT ok with). In time, we discovered this child LOVES horror movies and has been watching them since they were about 9 years old. Sympathy... The child wanted us to feel bad for them so lied. The child DID get to go to the movies for their birthday, they DID get to watch a horror film, but they DID love horror movies. The entire story was spun for manipulation.

We have had a child lie about us being abusers (thankfully told therapists ahead of time that they had plotted to do so) in order to hurt us because they were hurt by the discomforts of expectations in our home... manipulation. We have had a child tell other family lies about disciplines or rules in our home to achieve sympathy and connection... manipulation. We have had kids cry poor in order to be given inappropriate gifts... manipulation. We have had kids snuggle up to others in our lives in order to avoid responsibilities at home... manipulation.

All of these maladaptive ways in which a need for control shows up for adopted children can keep us from getting to know the authentic child underneath the behaviors. And as upsetting as some of the manipulations or demands may be for us to receive, we need to recognize that the behaviors are likely not about us. The behaviors exist because the child holds onto a fundamental belief that not being in control of the thing in their lives, mainly the relationships in their lives, will result in pain. Until we have proven ourselves safe AND the child has grown enough in their healing, the child is expected to feel a need for control and we must not internalize it as the child being naughty. The child is doing what they believe they must, until they know differently.

HOW CAN YOU HELP?

1. There is no such thing as too much love in the life of any child. The adopted child in your life needs your unconditional love as much as the next. Do not withhold love because you don't yet truly know the child or you suspect that you are on the receiving end of desires for control. Love doesn't require you to validate motive. Love doesn't require you to know or even like a child. Love requires you to show up accepting of how they are in this moment and simply hold space in your heart and life for them the best you can.

2. Take notes over time. The parents of every adoptive child are on a journey of discovery with their adopted child in which they are peeling back the layers similar to peeling off the layers of an onion. It can take YEARS for an adoptive parent that is well equipped to really feel like they know the core of who their child is. The fact that people outside of the parent relationship don't know the child yet, would be normal and expected. It isn't a reflection on you as a support person in the life of an adoptive child. It is a reflection on the time and space needed to establish a consistent relationship that allows the child to show up more authentically over time.

3. Validate the child and NOT what they are saying or doing. If a child is manipulating, you don't want to reinforce the behaviors. If a child is acting in fight/flight responses, you don't want to reinforce those behaviors. If the child is in a honeymoon and only feels accepted when they are "perfect" or "snuggly" as in a superficially attached kiddo, these

are behaviors we don't want to reinforce. Sending verbal and body language messages to trauma kids that say "I accept you if you are perfect or imperfect" or "I accept you snuggly or distant" will help the child to show up more authentic over time. A child in fight, flight, freeze, faun should not be judged for the way they handle their discomforts. The great news for family and friends of adoptive families is that the responsibility to train the child with healthy and helpful regulation skills doesn't fall on the friend or family. The adoptive parents and the specialists in the adopted child's life are far more trained in the unique needs of this trauma kid. Simply disconnecting from the behavior and recognizing it isn't about you, it is about the child, can help you not go into judgement around the child and their maladaptive ways.

4. Do not allow the child to put down their adoptive parents to you. I know… I know. Everyone needs a place to vent and yet every adopted child can make a list of the ways that the parent they didn't get to choose fails them and their hopes/expectations. Rather than entertaining what may be manipulations or complaints, I would ask you to turn them back to healthier options for conflict resolution. If a child has a valid concern with their parents, advise them to take the concern to their parents themselves or their therapist. I recognize speaking to the adoptive parents may be extra challenging and yet, in order to credit or discredit those concerns, it has to happen. If the child states that they have already expressed their concerns to their parent, tell them you intend to ask them when the parent comes to pick them up. The exception to this rule is if you believe that abuse is occurring in

which case you must call the child protection hotline rather than to endanger the child seeking your help. Whenever possible, limit complaint sessions and critical comments by asking what is going well in their lives or setting a boundary that you won't entertain gripe sessions, only legitimate safety concerns.

5. If the adopted child seems like an angel when they are with you, but you hear stories that are quite opposite from the parents, know that incongruence in the behavior of adopted children is very, very common. The original wound of all adoptees is from a birth mom. It is the greatest wound a child can suffer and because of that, adoptive moms particularly come under harsh criticism from adoptees. Adoptive parents have a lot of parenting, protecting, teaching, nurturing, enforcing boundaries and more that they are responsible for and many adoptees really struggle to accept the adoptive parents and their ways.

CHAPTER 7

ADOPTED CHILDREN ARE NOT LUCKY

I will never forget the time my son was told he was lucky to be adopted by us the first time. With his permission, I will give you some of his background.

My son lived in Ethiopia. He was in an orphanage from the age of 10 onward. He had attempted to help his biological mother, whom he dearly loved, stumble to the main road in town. He lived in the countryside where there were no medical services and his mother had become ill. She was so weak that she couldn't walk on her own to the road where she hoped to get a ride to the clinic. My son was about 6 years old when he had tried to support her on her walk to the road. His mother collapsed and died practically in his arms. His efforts to save her didn't pay off.

She was a single mom. My son's father had left them when he was much younger and ran off with another woman. Upon the death of his mother, my son was placed into an orphanage near their little village until his biological father could be located. Once his father was located, he was given to his father and his step mother in yet another town.

My son went to live with his father whom loved him. His father hadn't looked in on him while he was with his biological mother but was willing and able to care for him after the orphanage located him. My son believed things would be ok despite his grief and loss. However, his father drove a truck and delivered supplies all across Ethiopia. His father was gone days at a time which left him alone with his stepmother and the little half-sister they had created in their life before him entering the home.

The stepmother hated my adoptive son. When she looked at my son all she could see was the woman that her now husband had been with years before. She was jealous of the relationship prior to her. She hated my son's biological mother and resented that my adoptive son was now in their lives. She didn't want her husband to give money, time, or affection to this "foreigner" in her home. The abuse done unto him is beyond mentioning. It was after years of abuse that the neighbors were convinced that this adoptive son of mine would be murdered if he remained in the home and told an orphanage director of his existence and the abuse. About this time, the biological father passed and the abuses became even more deadly... now with zero protections in place that the father would provide between road trips. At age 10, my adoptive son was a double orphan with an abusive stepmother and then placed in an orphanage.

Fast forward to age 16 when my son finally made it to the US and into our home. He survived the death of the 2 people he had loved the most. He survived physical and emotional abuses. He even survived his own suicide attempts. He had lived through 2 orphanages. He had been stigmatized by society as "worthless" due to his orphan status and his struggles in school. He had to take on a second language and a whole new culture. He gave up the comforts of his culture and was forced to find his way in a fast-paced, success-redefined culture in the US. In the face of ALL OF THIS, he was still a sweet and caring young man.

An adoption worker had to come to our home to inspect our home prior to the adoption and to do a confidential interview with my soon-to-be adoptive son. He was nearly 18 years old at this time and the clock was ticking on the ability to get him adopted as a minor. We were all eager to get this visit behind us so that the courts could get the paperwork done.

The social worker came. The property was walked top to bottom. My adoptive son was taken into a private area in a living room to talk about any safety concerns he may have or any desires against the proposed adoption that he may not feel free to share in front of his adoptive father and me. The social worker and this precious young man came out and sat in the living room with me as we closed the meeting. She stands up and shakes my hand as she prepares to leave and then the words she spoke... they haunt me.

"You are so lucky to be adopted by this family."

Pause.

Go back and read that again. (Yes, I mean it.)

Lucky... I escorted the social worker out and then sat on the couch with tears in my eyes because it hadn't even registered yet for my son, though it had hit me harder than a mallet to my skull.

I sat knee to knee with a survivor and explained my horror... I was the lucky one if anyone here was to be described as "lucky". I had a living biological mother and father. I had never been abused. I always had a meal on my table. I had never even thought about taking my own life. I had never had to learn a new culture. I had never had to give up my favorite foods, smells, or comforts. I had toys as a child. I had education from the start. I had PBS teaching me my

ABC's and medical care for our entire family from the time I was born. I had clean water. I had consistent electricity. I had never had worms and I had never faced the stigma of my status in society. And yet here I was being told that my son whom had NEVER had a fraction of any of that was called the "lucky" one. I was sad. I was angry. I felt sick. My son saw my grief and also realized his own grief as we just held each other.

I do understand the intention of this social worker was to complement our family and was meant as a comparison to where my son was before he came into our family. The social worker's intention was good. She was a sweet and affirming woman whom mis-spoke in a way that had inadvertently caused a tremendous amount of pain for my son and I.

Adoption circumstances are ALWAYS born out of tragedy and loss. Assuming that a child will feel blessed, lucky, or even happy in their new home, because in the eyes of "the world" it is "better" than their old home, is simply not always the case. The older a child is, the less likely it will be the case at all, even if the child was adopted at birth. Each child needs the freedom to interpret both their past and their present as they see them, regardless of what others may or may not see. My adoptive son should have had a healthy mom who was cared for by his father rather than left to die under the care of her six-year-old son. My adoptive son shouldn't have been in a situation with a step-mother that was deadly. This young man was fortunate to be alive, let alone in our home but had every reason to be sad, angry, confused, and hurt instead of feeling "lucky". My son's very nature is one to see his blessings even in hardship so he was able to move past the social worker's comment much easier than many other adoptive kids can. And yet, the insensitivity of the comment happens OFTEN.

Many adoptive parents don't know what to say when told "your son is so lucky" so they say things like:

"We are the lucky ones."

"That is very nice of you."

"I'd say we are all blessed."

"He is loved."

All of these responses are made from a position of trying to humbly move past the comment. We adoptive parents are hot messes just like the rest of all moms out there. We are trying our best but have children with unique needs due to unique life experiences. To be praised for adopting is confusing. To have our kids told they are "lucky" to be adopted is confusing. In the confusion around the comments (remembering that they are almost always well intentioned when said), we try to smile and quickly, humbly move past them.

HOW CAN YOU HELP?

1. Avoiding statements in front of adopted children that assign them as being "lucky" or "blessed" helps the adoptive family to not have to wrestle with the incongruencies of the statements with their own life experiences.

2. Instead use statements like:

   "You have a beautiful family."

   "It's a pleasure to meet your family."

   "You are a loved child."

3. Oftentimes children that are adopted just want to be seen as children in a family, like any other child. Large adoptive families where kids are close in age, ethnicities vary, etc create, can rob children of the

ability to not be "labeled" as adoptive. Consider if it is necessary to even acknowledge the adoption in front of the children. Perhaps saving your curiosities for a private moment with just the parents would be best.

4. Family and friends may be in awe of the story that God is writing in the life of the adoptee in their world and want to freely announce it to others. This should be avoided in order to allow the child to share their story in their timing when the case of the child. Let the child and the adoptive parents be the ones to share the necessary details to others. Obviously if you are asked in a public setting with the child in your presence, you will want to frame your relationship in a way that you should previously discuss with the adoptive parent and child.

CHAPTER 8

ADOPTION TRAUMA LOOKS
DIFFERENT AT DIFFERENT AGES

Some of the information in this section can be hard to read without having a reaction to. It may be hard to understand the reasons for your family members or friends wanting to adopt. Can I please take this chance to remind you, as the reader, that adoption is by far the greatest gift I have received other than my spouse? The saying "no good thing comes easy" may be completely appropriate in this case. The below information is not to be weaponized as reasons NOT to adopt. These children NEED adoptive homes and yet it doesn't make adoption easy or painless for parents or children.

Adopted children have what is known as "adoption trauma". Trauma, for the sake of therapeutic discussion, is the cognitive, emotional, or physical differences experienced by a person due to an adverse event. Adoption trauma is when the biophysiological changes in a child are due to the removal of a child from their birthmother. Yes, even babies placed for adoption at birth have trauma wounds. We know that a baby experiences life within the womb for about 9 months and that in that time, the baby knows its mother. Upon birth he knows her smell, he knows her feelings, knows her body chemistry, her voice, and the very beat of her heart and the sound of her voice (*1). In the normal development of all infants, it isn't until age 6-9 months that a baby actually realizes that they are surrounded by their own skin and are not in fact a part of their mom (*2). Separating from the source of both their identity and their life at birth, does impact the life of a child in a way that leaves long-term repercussions.

Infants placed for adoption are twice as likely to need mental health help in their life (*3). Substance abuse rates for these babies are substantially higher (*4). Even suicide risks are four times higher than a non-adopted infant (*5). With statistics like these, adoption may seem cruel. And though it is not God's design for any child to be born into a situation that requires adoption as an answer (Matthew 18:2-6), adoption is merciful compared to a life of abuse, abandonment, neglect or even death. These statistics are mild compared to statistics for a child that endures trauma AFTER birth and at the hands of a birth parent that isn't stable.

Children that remain with their birth parents and go on to live a life characterized by instability develop something called Cumulative Harm Affect. The CDC partnered with Kaiser Permanente in 1995 and 1997 to both identify and quantify the effects of children living in abusive and/or neglectful environments (*6). This study was instrumental in understanding the long term impact of adverse childhood experiences in the home. There were 12 measures of abuse and neglect that were tallied and scores were given for each one of the 12 measures. The study found that a child with more points had exponential risk (hugely so at 4 or more points) of negative impacts in their adult lives. Consequences to these children as adults like domestic violence, divorce, addiction, and mental health disorders may be more logical for us to predict. But would it surprise you that needing eye glasses, developing inflammatory based diseases, COPD, and even cancer are far more likely for children raised in adverse homes?

Why is all of this important to understand? It can be scary to accept as an adoptive parent, let alone a family, friend, or professional engaging with the child or family. It doesn't mean the child is "broken" or "doomed". After the repeated findings of this above referenced study, and subsequent adapted but similar ones, scientists immediately began looking for ways to "undo" the short and long term effects of childhood trauma (this includes adoption trauma). Though there is no pill, no therapist, no "quick fix" for any of the pains our society's little treasured people endure, there are interventions that have been found effective. Don't be afraid to both accept and love an adoptee! They are priceless, didn't choose the circumstances they were born into, and they NEED your love to reach their highest potential.

What You May See

Babies with trauma can appear either super easy going and rarely cry, or they can cling to their adoptive parents and be super sensitive and needy. Toddlers can have bigger mood swings, more physical outburst, withdrawal from strangers or stressors, or be obstinate at a higher level. School-aged kids can have learning difficulties, social differences, perceived over or under attachment to adults in their lives, and intense behaviors indicating a desire to be in control. Teens can show greater rebellion, fall into addiction, or even become withdrawn and suicidal. None of these things are guaranteed and adopted children may breeze through any phase of development with zero signs of trauma. These wounds can present in any of the stages of development, regardless of previously normal phases.

How Can You Help?

1. As hard as it may be, don't take behaviors personally. Behaviors that are extreme or don't match the situation are not personal despite how they feel. The maladaptive actions and attitudes of adoptees are rooted in trauma and the biophysiological changes that have occurred within their bodies. Recognize that the child needs love, healing, and maturity far more than the child needs rejection or judgement.

2. Don't try to take on a role that isn't yours. When we see a child hurting, we want to help them heal. When we see a child out of control, we want to discipline. When we see a child running onto a train track, we want to drive onto the track and stop the train. Family, friends, and others in the lives of adoptees have 2 jobs:

   a. To love them with boundaries that reinforce healthy and helpful interactions

   b. To show up stable and consistent

   No amount of love heals a child. It is God's job to be the Healer, the Way Maker, and the Miracle worker. We have to let God be God, and us be us.

3. Accept that the adoptive parents are doing the best they can with the knowledge and resources they have. If you have never adopted then you simply have no idea what it is like to wake up to the task of raising a child that has needs greater than what you as a parent could ever meet. Grace is what adoptive parents need, not unasked for advice or judgement. Asking how you can help is always a good thing, yet often times, adoptive parents don't know what they need to help them or the circumstances.

*1 https://babyschool.yale.edu/does-my-baby-recognize-me/
*2 AAP. 2021. Emotional and social development in babies: Birth to 3 months. American Academy of Pediatrics. https://www.healthychildren.org/English/ages-stages/baby/pages/Emotional-and-Social-Development-Birth-to-3-Months.aspx [Accessed February 2022]
*3 https://www.ncbi.nlm.nih.gov/pmc/articles/PMC4475346/
*4 https://www.ncbi.nlm.nih.gov/pmc/articles/PMC3499473/
*5 https://www.ncbi.nlm.nih.gov/pmc/articles/PMC3784288/
*6 https://www.cdc.gov/violenceprevention/aces/index.html

CHAPTER 9

SECONDARY TRAUMA

Primary trauma is defined as duress that occurs due to direct exposure to a traumatic event either through victimization or the witnessing of it. Secondary trauma is defined as the emotional duress that results when an individual hears about or witnesses the consequences of the firsthand trauma experiences of others. Because adopted children have adoption trauma, often times the adoptive parents end up in what is known as a trauma cycle.

Let's use an example of a boy named John. John was 3 when his mother's boyfriend would come home drunk every morning as he started to wake up. In the beginning, John would be in the kitchen scouring the cabinets for food to eat. When the boyfriend would enter, John would be accused of making noise and being disruptive in his search for food and then be beaten. This experience taught John to lay in bed awake until the boyfriend got home and passed out on the sofa. Once the house was asleep, John would again go looking for food. Since John was only 3, He often had soiled diapers that were soggy and stinky. He would push chairs up to the counter and climb up to search in the "secret" cabinet above the fridge where his mom would hide the cheese crackers so he couldn't get them all at once. Unknowingly, John would get feces on the kitchen counter and get beaten regularly for dirtying the counter tops. This taught John to take off his diapers when they were soiled which only led to carpets being soiled instead. Again, John would be beaten. A starved, beaten, scared version of John was removed from his biological mom and her boyfriend. He was eventually placed for adoption.

John's adoptive parents were both angry and grieved when they heard his story. Adoptive dad stated that he was thankful the boyfriend was unknown because he would want to beat the daylights out of the man. Adoptive mom was so grieved she felt ill because it was unimaginable to her that a woman whom had given birth to a hungry child would actually hide the only food in the home. John was the person with primary trauma in this example. Adoptive mom and dad were the people with secondary trauma in this example. Though the adoptive parents had never even met the two care givers in John's life, they had very big feelings about the biological mom's and boyfriend's actions.

After John had settled into his new adoptive home, the adoptive parents would correct John, asking him to leave a diaper on. They also worked hard to make sure he never felt soiled since he was too emotionally young to potty train. Every time adoptive parents would correct John and put the diaper back on that John would remove, John would get physically violent toward his adoptive parents. When John would attempt to climb onto the counters or on top of the adoptive family's refrigerator, the family would calmly put him down to the ground. John would use profanity and bite at adoptive mom's hands as she attempted to keep John safe. Mom and dad remained calm the first many times they were attacked by John but eventually, the adoptive parents began raising their voices in an attempt to divert the aggressive behaviors and even slapped little John's hands. John reacted with fear and shame at first but then started getting louder, more aggressive, and more out of control. The trauma cycle had overtaken the home. The adoptive parents didn't feel good about how they were parenting but were exhausted and had tried everything they knew while John didn't seem to get any better. John was untrusting of his new parents from the beginning. His adoptive parents, acting loud and physically aggressive, just reinforced the ideas John had about adults being scary and unsafe. Not getting loud didn't work. Not getting physical didn't work. Nothing seemed to work.

Trauma Cycle

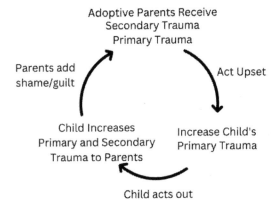

When people that love the parents of adoptive children see the trauma cycle playing out in the lives of their loved ones, relatives and friends are hurt watching those they love be hurt in the process of parenting. As an adoptive mother, one of the hardest things I have experienced that was unexpected was the ways in which my parents, in-laws, friends, and church family would hurt because of the dynamics in our home. I knew my husband and I had made a decision that would come with difficulties for us. I failed to fully understand that our difficulties would simultaneously create difficulties for those we loved outside of our home.

Some of our children didn't come to Jason and I until they were teenagers. Teens are hard. Trauma teens are even harder. The behaviors some of our kids displayed were pretty unimaginable. I was called things much more horrific than just profanities and truly, they weren't deserved. I never hit my kids. I very, very rarely raised my voice at them. I was imperfect and certainly undereducated and ill-equipped 15 years ago when I first brought in an older child, but I was loving, patient, and committed. My children needed more and at the time, I took it personally. I was wounded. I was afraid. I was enrolled in every service I could find for our family and it all felt like failure at every turn. I was broken and in survival mode. My family knew it. My parents wanted to help me fix it. My mother loved me and accepted my choices, but it pained her to watch us live in a hurting home and not have any solutions for us on how to make it better. My mother experienced secondary trauma because of our family. My father experienced secondary trauma. Those we love the most outside of our home were deeply wounded by the things our family had endured.

Primary and secondary trauma affects siblings within adoptive homes as well. It is very hard for adoptive parents and outsiders looking in to accept that children that were not abandoned, abused, or neglected end up with trauma in their lives that could have been prevented if the adoptive parents had simply chosen not to adopt. A child innocent of the trauma cycle can get engulfed and be left with secondary trauma wounds of resentment as they watch their parents experience pain at the hands of their adopted siblings. The siblings get primary trauma from the maladaptive behaviors that are thrown directly at them as the adoptee attempts to find their way in life. And yet, what Jason and I have found as our kids have become adults, is that children are far more resilient than one would think when there is loving leadership in the home that establishes a level of safety and expectation between siblings. Our adopted children may have had some jealousy or resentment around circumstances between siblings during childhood, but they love each other fiercely and the wounds between siblings are far less than the amounts of love between them now.

Much of our family outside our home doesn't accept many of our children as their kin. Loud behaviors and unsafe conduct can really make it hard for people to unconditionally accept a child into their family and lives. Watching their family that is loved (like Jason and myself) be treated in unloving, hurtful ways can be hard to forget or overcome. Secondary trauma to onlookers and extended family is very painful and real.

How You Can Help

1. Be ready to identify primary and secondary trauma as you are exposed to adoption. When you see that you are struggling with intense feelings that linger, seek help for your own trauma so that it isn't lasting and can be set down with little consequence.

2. No child chooses or wants to have adoption trauma. No adoptee wants to inflict primary or secondary wounds into the relationships around them. A child is just that… a child. There is no maturity, no complex reasoning skills, no rooted understandings of why they have maladaptive behaviors or even the fact that they do, in many cases. Recognizing that behaviors are usually reactive and that the trauma creating the

behaviors is unresolved aren't concepts a child understands. Understanding the root cause of the behaviors and the immaturity at play within the child will help you forgive and move through the trauma now brought into the adoptive home. Handling your own trauma experiences and accepting that the adoptive family is doing the best they can will help you to handle all of those in healthy and helpful ways.

3. Try, where you can, to not hold the behaviors of a traumatized child against them for longer than you must. Consider seeking a deeper understanding of the ways a body is impacted by trauma and how those wounds from the past get stored in the body.

If you had childhood trauma of our own, be sure to address what is historic for you versus what is currently happening. Traumatic or stressful circumstances of today can bring up events or times in the past that felt similar. If you are drudging up emotions and memories as you are dealing with the adoptee in your circle, make sure you don't react to the adoptive child in ways that aren't earned in real time. Work hard not to project your past onto the life of the child. Work hard not to place feelings or thoughts from your past onto the child as though they should feel the same as you did. That can be wounding and inappropriate to the adoptee.

CHAPTER 10

COCOONING IS NORMAL

So now you understand that every baby born unto her mother already knows and is attached to their biological mom. They begin developing their sense of smell late into the first trimester. The smell of the mother's womb, the sound of the mother's voice, even the emotional changes of their mom have all created impact on this baby. Suddenly, the baby is born and despite believing that they are indeed one flesh with their biological mother, they are separated from the only human they have depended on, known, and trusted to this point. Either the birth mom has chosen to place their baby for adoption as a selfless act of love toward the new baby, ensuring that every ounce of stability and security that bio mom cannot provide is met. Or the baby is taken away from the biological mother due to the mother being seen as unfit. Either way, this baby is traumatized and believes that it has lost a part of itself.

When a baby or young child is placed into an adoptive home, many adoptive mothers choose to "cocoon" with their adoptee. Cocooning is a term adoptive parents use for wrapping their baby into a secure, isolated environment in order to bond, adjust, and eventually fly like a butterfly would upon breaking out of their cocoon. Some moms don't want others to hold the baby for the first weeks or months of the child being placed into their family. They want to establish a clear difference and connection between themselves as the adoptive mother and the other people in the child's life. Other moms will allow the child to be held or even engaged for short periods of time only. Some adoptive parents won't even leave the home for the first few months in order that the child can get a clear connection with his home and parents. Cocooning can involve wearing a baby during the day, co-sleeping at night, and even choosing to leave a baby on the bottle or with a pacifier longer than normal.

How You Can Help

1. Accepting an adoptive parent's desire to cocoon above your desire to connect with the new child is a must. The intentions of the adoptive mother are not to withhold opportunity for you to love their new child. The intentions are simply to make sure that given the size of the trauma wound their adoptee has, the wound is cared for properly before the child moves on to accepting the relationships outside of the parent-child relationship.

2. Some people truly get disgusted when seeing a baby worn all day or a bottle in the mouth of a 16 month old. I want to encourage you to set aside preconceived ideas about what is "right". If a parent has taken the time to understand attachment, adoption trauma, and if they have done all the licensing requirements to be eligible to adopt, then they are making an informed decision about the techniques that they are using in raising their new adoptee. Accepting their parenting strategies without judgement allows the adoptive family to feel safe sharing the unique needs of their adopted child with you.

CHAPTER 11

SAVE THE STORIES

Jason and I were so excited to become adoptive parents. We had struggled with infertility and adoption was a definite answer to prayer and a clear calling by the time we had gotten our license. Licensing in the state of Arizona required a class that would take place many Saturdays. In those classes, we heard many adoption testimonials and many tragic stories of children that had come into state custody. The stories were shared for the purpose of adoptive parents growing in understanding and skills to best support the child that would be placed into our family.

Outside of our adoption classes, when people heard we were planning to grow our family through adoption, responses would vary. Some people wanted to tout us as being saints for taking in a child that had different DNA than ours. As mentioned before, this is uncomfortable for adoptive parents as we certainly are not trying to be saints and our kids won't see us as anything close to saints. Some people would be inquisitive wondering the cost, length of process, reasons why we opted to adopt. Others would go into story telling mode almost immediately.

Almost everyone knows at least one adopted child. Some people know of famous adoptive parents or adoptees. Others know stories from reunion shows with adult adoptees meeting their biological parents for the first time as seen on daytime television. Then there are people who have seen families live through difficulties relating to adoption in their own families. I am not sure what the hope or intention is when a person dives into sharing adoption horror stories. Are they wanting adoptive parents to really count the cost of adoption and perhaps change our mind? Are they just fascinated by the story in itself so feel compelled to share this "fascinating" story of tragedy and pain? Are they hoping to education adoptive parents as to the worst case scenario of what can be expected? No matter the motive, can we simply ask that the stories be saved?

Going into adoption isn't for the faint of heart. The time, money, prayer, planning, paperwork, and logistics alone are enough to make any sane person's head spin. The fact any family does all that is necessary to be licensed and allowed to adopt is a miracle of sorts. Then the fact that any family is willing to go through all that is required for the privilege of adopting a child that is known to have trauma, tells you that it isn't just a decision based on logic but rather a decision made out of immense love for a child that they haven't yet met. (It is often times a reflection of a tremendous amount of love for the Lord and a response to His calling in scripture as well.) Stories that serve up the worst sides of adoption on a platter before prospective adoptive parents are not likely to change the course of adoption. Instead, these stories only give room for fear and anxiety to blossom where a certain amount already exists. In the life of an adoptive parent, this is by far the biggest thing they have done in life up until this point. The decision was not made lightly and the full realm of the costs of the decision have already been weighed. If as family and friends you cannot support the decision to adopt, can you at least accept the decision? Can you reserve your personal stories, doubts, and fears in order to show acceptance to the adoptive family in the making?

How You Can Help

1. Look honestly at your personal feelings and opinions as they relate to the idea of adoption. Are you willing to adjust those opinions and your expectations? How can the people you know that are adopting and you both benefit by your willingness to be open and accepting?

2. If you have stories to share can you consider if you are sharing them for your benefit or the benefit of the adoptive family? If the adoptive family will not benefit by the sharing of the story, would you consider keeping it to yourself?

CHAPTER 12

THE FINANCIAL COSTS OF ADOPTION

This is another section that is honestly challenging for me to write. Why does the cost of adoption matter to anyone other than the adoptive parents? Yet, there is both a lot of curiosity around the cost of adoption by those that are at arm's length and criticisms. The need to address this topic exists.

Oh how ignorant Jason and I were when we went into adoption as it related to finances. We had been open to a birth parent adoption or the adoption of a younger child in the beginning. We knew that if we were matched with a birth parent placement, we would pay upwards of $13,000 for the adoption expenses (that number is significantly higher now). We also knew that if we were placed with a child in the custody of the state, we would be eligible for a small subsidy payment as well as health insurance until the child was 18 years old. In our minds, adoption was more affordable than the midwife and birthing center we had once hoped to have a biological child at, or at least close. In the event of state placed children, we saw it as being blessed with a child while receiving added benefits to support raising our adoptee to the best of our financial abilities.

Now nearly 20 years into the world of adoption, I can firmly state that adoption was the most expensive adventure we have ever embarked on. Adopted children that have exposure to drugs/alcohol in utero have more needs than those that do not. Adopted children with post birth traumas have higher risk factors than those placed directly after birth. My children all have high risk factors for their adolescent years. These risk factors make free educational options less optimal. My children's unique needs have required services well outside the realm of what insurance will cover, both the state given insurance and that in which we subscribe to through my husband's work. My children don't reach maturity at the "average" age and require supports longer than most biological children.

Our finances are exactly that... ours. It is easy from the outside looking in to see the financial impact of any one of our given children in a season and simply think we should "quit" on the adoption or let the child have the free (though far below adequate) services that state insurance will cover. It would be easy to look at our net worth and question the justice for our children that are more typical in development (because they didn't cost an arm and a leg in added mental health services or educational services) as we imagine what splitting up the remaining assets will look like upon our passing. It would be easy to look at money invested in helping a child that appears to have no tangible healing or return on the investment and think that it is foolish to spend money where it simply isn't "worth it". In the case of international adoptions or the bringing of our children from Africa, it may be easy for others to simply wonder why we would need to invest the money in a child from overseas when "affordable" kids are right here in our home state.

I understand the logic in questioning the financial spending of adoptive parents. Logic, once again, isn't the ruling factor. People buy fancy cars for $70,000 and don't feel the need to justify it. People take extravagant trips and are the envy of social media. When people are spending money on things that "feel good", it seems no logic is needed. Yet when we as people are compelled to invest our resources into the lives of a hurting child, some will judge the spending preferring to see us buy a luxury sedan rather than "throw money away" at therapeutic or educational supports for our adopted children. Either we adoptive parents are seen as "foolish" or as "saints". Neither is true. Adoptive parents that are investing financial resources in their children are simply acting in accordance with their personal moral compass. In my case, I can look in the mirror at night if I know that I have done all that I possibly can do to help my child reach their highest potential, regardless of the outcome. I spend money simply trying to help my child to be the best version of themselves while they are still a minor. I feel it is my job to provide opportunities for my kids, regardless of their ability or willingness to fully embrace what is offered. I have to try my best, and let them show me otherwise.

I have had family ask me to spend more money on myself, our home updating, or vacations with Jason and myself. I get it. They want to see me be "okay" and don't understand that I am the most "okay" I will ever be when I know my kids have the best chance of being "okay" for themselves. No trip, no yard upgrades, no cruises, can do for my heart and soul what the healing of my child can.

How Can You Help?

1. Acceptance. You may not understand the financial spending that goes into adoption or that comes in supporting the growth of the adoptee. Understanding isn't a necessary component of acceptance. Acceptance comes from a willingness to allow the

adoptive family to be autonomous with their finances, parenting decisions, disciplines, and growth.

2. Don't give unless it can be done freely. Many adoptive parents fundraise or ask for support from loved ones for things like therapeutic boarding programs if they are needed. It is always a blessing to receive the financial support of friends and family as God calls parents into big things. However, if giving will come with resentment over the adoption process or the services provided, it is better to simply not give in the first place. A family struggling with trauma in their home doesn't need the added pressure of pleasing the supporters/donors with each decision that is made on behalf of their adopted child. If you can give freely and with a trust for the person in charge of spending the donated funds, then giving in a mutual blessing.

3. Adopting children means having children with different needs. Some kids will do better with a trade school than a traditional college. Some kids will need more therapeutic finances and supports. It is hard for adoptive families to reconcile why some grandparents or extended family want to help fund college or therapies for some kids, but not others. As a supporter of an adoptive family, try to understand that adoptive parents want all of the children in their family to feel equally supported and loved. If you are looking to financially support any children in an adoptive home, consider if you can support all of the children in equitable ways. If you cannot support them all in ways that feel congruent to the children, please discuss this with the adoptive parents before being generous with any one of the children.

CHAPTER 13

THE COMPARISON TRAP

What is your favorite hamburger joint? Why? What makes one burger taste better than another? What is better about one bun or secret sauce? Comparison is at the heart of our value system and isn't wrong. Though it isn't wrong, it may not be helpful in all cases.

When a woman gets pregnant, she often tracks the development of her fetus online or in a book to see what normal development of the baby within her is. The actual development of the baby is then measured at obstetric appointments. This typically doesn't end just because the baby is born.

Kids are measured against their peers from the very beginning and it is a normal way in which our society determines the healthy development of a child. Intake forms at doctor offices will ask how old a child was when they first sat independently. The forms will ask the child's age at first speaking and at toileting. Many forms will ask the age the child stopped bedwetting. Once our child is in elementary school, teachers will compare the reading, speech, social skills, and behavior of each child to what is "normal" for kids of the same age.

This book is largely about comparing adopted children to those that are not. Comparisons will exist in the minds and hearts of those around us. We are even self-critical from an early age when we begin to recognize that some girls have hair we would "rather have" or that some kids get gifts at Christmas that are more preferred than ours. Comparison isn't the problem, what we do with our comparisons of our adopted children to same age peers or siblings, is what determines if our comparisons are hurtful.

Statistics don't lie. Adopted children have medical, social, academic, and behavioral differences than same aged peers if we look broadly at the population group. That being said, each child will have strengths and weaknesses comparatively to others in both their adoptive peer group and the nonadoptive peer group. Where we run into frequent issues in the work that I do is when parents use comparison to try to motivate their adopted child or friends/family of adoptees attempt to avoid embarrassment as they engage with the world around them with the adopted child in their lives by explaining away the differences.

Adopted children often act younger than their physical age. They can toilet later than same aged peers. It can be embarrassing for a grandmother of an adopted child to drop off their grandson at the church Sunday School still wearing Pull-Ups at age 6 so it is explained away in front of the child which creates shame. An adopted child may want to carry a blanket until they are 14 or 15 years old. Asking the child if her friends "still carry their blankie" is likely to create shame where a child already struggles with feeling different and misunderstood. Or how about the child that sucks their fingers until they are 12 years old because they have sensory needs that are unmet and developmentally are stunted? The child likely wants to stop sucking their finger and yet hasn't found a way to do so. Comparing won't motivate the child out of the behavior. Instead the shame will only cause secondary behaviors.

In working with adopted children and raising my own, I always try to frame their differences as accepted and point out strengths. Of course they see this as mom being mom. I also try to hear them and validate their feelings and struggles around their own perception of differences. I work hard not to point out differences that they have yet to realize. As the kids get older, they become more aware of their differences and often with time, the gap between the adopted child's development and the same-age peer only increases. This can be very hard for the kids to accept. Low self-esteem plagues adopted kids and this is just one of the many reasons why. It is so hard for everyone who loves the adopted child or the child with disabilities to watch a beautiful, perfectly-imperfect child fall into levels of self-hatred. Combine the low view of self with hormones or chemically induced depression, you can see that the teen years can be very complex and difficult for the adopted child to navigate.

How Can You Help?

1. When possible, rather than complimenting the child with gaps in development or social/emotional differences, help them to see their own successes by asking them to tell you how they accomplished the things they did that day. Allowing our adopted children to see their own successes through the lens of their own words is more powerful than compliments.

2. Compliments can backfire with adopted children. Adopted children can feel like a fraud that has "pulled one over on you" if you don't see them the way they see themselves. Asking questions that lead to positive

self-discovery is the best approach. Also asking how you can help them to feel pretty, feel smart, or feel accepted can be useful though they sometimes don't have answers.

3. Avoid all shaming remarks rooted in comparing the adopted child to peers of a similar age. The path for each child is different and embracing those differences from the top down will help a child not to fall into self-judgement.

4. Some children "puff" as though they have fantastic self-esteem when in all reality, the size of their "puff" is comparable to the size of the hole in their hearts created by low self-worth. They work hard to not be wounded bigger by trying to convince others how great they are. A safe approach is to validate that they don't have to be perfect or the best at any given thing, and that just being themselves is enough, without contradicting their bragging.

CHAPTER 14

VARIED ETHNICITIES AND CULTURES

We live in a world that is racially charged. Some locations act more on racial or cultural differences than others, yet since the beginning of time, it seems humanity is simply judgmental and cruel of ethnic (and other) differences.

Jason and I travel to Ethiopia for missions regularly. In Ethiopia, everyone indigenous to the country is black. There are varied facial features, different shades of black and certainly different textures of hair amongst Ethiopians. That being said, even in a country that is all comprised of black men and women, racism exists. Because the differences are primarily by tribe (again, they are all black so technically we don't use racism to describe the disputes) it is called tribalism. Regardless of what it is called, people get killed for the region in which they belong in Ethiopia. Certain colors of "black" are considered "more beautiful" than others as are certain hair textures.

Asia is no exception. South America, Europe, Australia---indigenous people groups, tribal differences, skin color differences, sexual orientation preferences, religious beliefs, and more are used to divide and judge humans all over the world. Our adopted children will be no different.

Adopted children are a subcategory in our culture. Simply because they are adopted, the culture knows that the children in question had parents that either chose not to raise them, or had parents that weren't allowed to raise them. This stigmatizes the children and the biological parents. Those very stigmas can be weaponized as a means for peers and adults to either intentionally or unintentionally be cruel or demeaning to adopted children.

Because my children vary in race and cultural heritage, it is literally like all of our family members are wearing signs on their foreheads as we enter public places. Some of my children think their sign reads "Adopted and proud to be loved". Others of my children think their signs read "My other mom chose drugs over me". Yet another child may think their sign reads "These parents aren't as amazing as you might think." Finally, another's may read "Please don't ask. Just let me be a kid." Can you see how depending on age, history, and confidence, a child's sign may change over the years? And can you see how unfair it is to a child for them to always have to wear a sign?

I remember when Jason and I first began growing our family for adoption. We had three babies under 18 months old and all three had different colored skin. We would be in a restaurant and the servers would just look puzzled. It was as if they were trying to rationalize how I could have been with 2 men before the one I was currently seated next to and popped out all of these babies. The confusion was a bit humorous... as if the old "milkman" joke had come to pass in our home. Regardless, the looks have changed but the children are now the teens that have had "those looks" and "those comments" their whole lives. I can't help but to wonder how much impact it really has had on their identity and self-confidence.

Respecting my children's heritage is also an important factor in our home. We have Native American children and have made efforts for them to both know that they are Native as well as to understand bits and pieces of what that means for their ancestry. We have Hispanic children that have been exposed to likely more Mexican food than they would prefer! And they have been to Mexico several times to better understand why their biological family chose to come to the US rather than remain in Mexico. We also have Ethiopian children that regularly attend a local Ethiopian church, enjoy the "injera" bread and sauces, and are fluent in their native language. As a family, we want our children to celebrate both their differences and their similarities. We work to remove shame from every arena of our home, but especially places where our kids had no choice in the things they are shamed for. Race is one of those places where society may invite shame in, but our home will choose to love beyond color, ability, heritage, age, religion, or sexual preference.

How Can You Help?

1. Some kids don't want to celebrate their heritage and some do. Respecting the child's position without pressure or guilt is important. Children looking to blend in will want to be seen as "the same" despite obvious differences and may not be ready to embrace their individuality in their ethnicity. Other children will see their color as a positive attribute and want it celebrated. Educate yourself where you can on the biological family's history and the heritage of the people group when possible for when your child is ready to learn more.

2. Some ways you can bring culture, heritage, and ethnicity into your home are through the foods, music, arts, traditions, and clothing of the child's ancestry. This can be very fun. Coffee ceremonies are a big part

of holidays in Ethiopia so we have the coffee cups and fixings to do the ceremonies in our home. Indian fry bread is delicious and we stop at stands when they are available. We love the rugs, baskets, songs, and clothing of other cultures and by embracing all cultures, our children are more ready to embrace their own culture.

3. Ask questions. Without implications, ask open ended questions that allow the adopted people in your life to express what it means to them to be of their color or culture. Allow the child to express what things they would like to do to honor their heritage and perhaps research ideas together.

CHAPTER 15

HOLIDAYS MAY NOT BE HAPPY

I remember being very confused after bringing in my first older child when Christmas rolled around and it was as hard as it turned out to be. My daughter was obviously excited to have the time off school and to have given Santa her wish list. She had anticipated that the Christmas tree would have plenty of gifts. I did have enough awareness to prepare her ahead of time ( ) as far as realistic expectations for the gifts, the guests, and the activities, and I mapped out a tentative time schedule. Despite this, Christmas was rough nearly every year. And it wasn't just Christmas. Most holidays were very hard.

Change in routine is hard for trauma exposed children. Sugar and food dye can be hard for our kids. Late nights, unexpected surprises (no matter how awesome they are), people rarely seen, and different expectations can all be triggers for dysregulated bodies. Holidays have split attention, a busyness in the air, excitement and foods at a whole new level... so it is no wonder that holidays can be challenging for kids thriving on routine and stability. Combine these things with the fact that holidays are largely shared with family and adopted children have complex family histories, deeply rooted familial questions regarding identity and more... holidays can simply be too much for even adopted adults to process, let alone adopted children.

Mother's Day is no exception when it comes to difficult holidays. Some of my children have 2 moms. I am the third mom to some of my children and to even another, I am mom number 4. I lost my mom in my mid-thirties. Mother's Day hasn't been easy since. Every year I am reminded of both how incredible my mom was AND how much I miss her. Sometimes I try to bargain with the Lord for just one more day of having my mom back in front of me to soak in her affection, wisdom, and unconditional love. If the relationship with my mom was so stable that my only regrets with my mom were a desire for more time, I can only imagine how much harder it must be for my children to set aside their own grief, confusion, fears, and pains in an attempt to celebrate ME as if I am their only mother. Mother's Day is far too complicated for most adopted children to really express outwardly. The result is often inward dysregulation that shows up as negative behaviors. These behaviors, though painful and hard to navigate, would be expected behaviors for adopted children.

How Can You Help?

1. Having grace for the entire adoptive family on holidays is a huge gift to the individuals within the family. Adoptive moms are just like other moms and try really hard to make holidays special for everyone involved. Though the efforts are there, the outcome of Mom's efforts is often beyond her control. Your unconditional love, grace, and making-the-best-of-it will go a long way.

2. If you have any unusually big surprises or changes in what is planned for an adoptive child, please consider notifying the adoptive parents in advance. Working with the adoptive parents to determine the best way

to present any unexpected events will help the child to have a more enjoyable day.

3. Wearing joy is a powerful weapon against hardship and anxiety. When you show up to holidays at ease and with a smile on your face, it is easier for the adoptive family to catch your vibe! Remember that any difficulties are not caused by you in most cases (,) so give yourself permission to relax and have fun whether the kiddo in your circle is having a good day or a hard day.

CHAPTER 16

PARENTING WILL LIKELY LOOK DIFFERENT

I remember the first time I was told that my child "needed a good spanking". My child had Failure to Thrive, was a feeding tube toddler, and we were in Las Vegas on vacation. We were walking from one resort to the other on The Strip. My daughter decided to walk next to the sidewalk, in the road where the drain gutter was. I told her "sidewalk please". She froze in place and hid her beautiful eyes under her hair, postured downward. I went to move her so she would be safe. From her frozen, shutdown state, she felt unsafe and began slapping at my hands and screaming in order to try to keep me from picking her up. It was quite a scene. It came out of nowhere and seemed unjustified. I am sure that in her head, she had a reason for what she was doing. Her speech delays and brain-processing differences made the circumstances impossible for me to understand. An onlooker decided that my response should be to spank my child for slapping at me.

I am sure there are times all through parenting my adopted children where family, friends, teachers, and onlookers felt that my ways of discipline or my expectations were not valid. I am ok with others not agreeing with my parenting. I believe most parents, adoptive or not, come under criticism for how they parent at times. That being said, adoptive parents that are under the teaching of adoption parenting books or therapists will look very different than "typical" or "old school" parents.

Because adopted children have trauma at the core, adoptive parenting should be body-based parenting rather than behavior-based parenting. Adoptive parenting should not involve spanking or any forms of physical punishment. The methods I teach for adoptive parenting in Journey University for Adoptive Families are 100% around requiring calm bodies in the home, from the parents down to the kids. I require withholding preferred activities when bodies are not calm and pair positive reinforcements throughout the day with kids that work hard to have safe, calm bodies and mouths. As you can see, this is a completely different parenting concept than what you likely have seen used for non-adopted children.

Some adoptive parents will sit with their kids during a time-out. Some adoptive parents will redirect a child to "walk away" when escalated rather than validate the topic the child is bringing them. Parenting adopted children is designed to meet sensory needs, neurological differences, attachment, developmental differences and more. It is take a tremendous amount of work for adoptive parents to understand the unique needs of their child and to consistently work to parent to meet those unique needs.

How Can You Help?

1. If you are not an adoptive parent, I want to encourage you to withhold judgement around the differences in the way the adoptive family you know and love is parenting. Uphold the instructions given to you by the adoptive parents when you are the person in charge of

the kids. Consistency is critical for the success of adoptive children in feeling safe and cared for. Because adopted children had another mother, they do question their adoptive parents at times. This questioning is normal but when others seem to question it as well, the child struggles even more with accepting their adoptive family.

2. Speak life over the adopted child and their adoptive family when in front of the child. If you have questions about the differences in parenting that you observe, it is ok to ask the questions but not in front of the child. You can always question, you are not expected to fully understand the methods used in parenting, but in the end your support is needed as the adoptive parents work to implement the researched and therapeutic strategies being used to parent their adoptee.

3. It is never ok for anyone to physically touch an adopted child in anger in any way. If you are with an adopted child and you are upset, hurt or frustrated please remove yourself from the cause of the frustration (while securing the child in a safe space) rather than placing your hand on the child in anger. As hard as it is to remain calm with your tone, even raising a voice can be triggering and bring up deeply rooted trauma wounds in an adoptee. Considering trauma kids tend to be reactive and can be difficult, remaining calm in the face of behaviors can be challenging. You are human and going to make mistakes. Educating yourself on regulation strategies to calm your body in the face of stress will only help you to navigate your relationship with the adopted child.

CHAPTER 17

CONCLUSION- BE LOVE

1 Corinthians 13:4-8a Love is patient and kind; love does not envy or boast; it is not arrogant or rude. It does not insist on its own way, it is not irritable or resentful; it does not rejoice at wrongdoing, but rejoices with the truth.

All children need love. Love is not an emotion as much as it is an action. When we put on love, we are choosing to be patient and kind. We are choosing to not make things about us or act on our emotions. We choose to patiently seek relationship with a child in need. We choose to wait out negative behaviors where we can. We choose to forgive the hurtful ways in which our hurting children present. We don't celebrate consequences, but seek truth to take victory in the hearts of all hurting kids. Children are so valuable, so precious, so priceless... and all children NEED an example of the unconditional love of Jesus Christ in their lives as much as the next person.

Raising trauma exposed, adopted children is a very difficult calling. It is one that most of society will never fully understand and that often leaves adoptive parents feeling alone, judged, hopeless, and afraid. But why? The lack of information that leads to a lack of understanding is the root cause of the misperceptions and judgements that cause adoptive families to lose family members, friendships, and support systems. Yes, adoption hurts. Life hurts. Adopted children didn't get a choice and we adults are blessed that we DO. We get to choose unconditional love. We get to choose safety. We choose health, stability, fun, purposed-living, and community.

If this book has been given to you by an adoptive parent, you have been invited to choose "LOVE" in the life of an adoptive family. If you have purchased this book, you have already chosen to be "LOVE" in the life of an adoptive family. Either way, standing with an adoptive child is important work. You are now more equipped to be steady, stable, and amazing in the life of a chosen child. May God bless you as you aim to make a difference in a child that is surely worthy. May you feel more empowered to be a source of positive influence as you move forward.